The
Mid-Life Crisis

The Brat

''ello, dis ees Tilda, woo are woo?'

The
Mid-Life Crisis

SOCIAL STEREOTYPES FROM THE
Telegraph magazine

Victoria Mather
and
Sue Macartney-Snape

JOHN MURRAY

For Christopher Fildes,
the diamond who's a girl's best friend
V.M.

For my younger set of godchildren,
James Korössy, Angus Macdonald, Natasha Hall
and Djazia Spowers, with love
S.M.-S.

Text © 2002, 2004 and 2005 Daily Telegraph plc
and Victoria Mather

Illustrations © 2002, 2004 and 2005 Daily Telegraph plc
and Sue Macartney-Snape

First published in Great Britain in 2005 by John Murray (Publishers)
A division of Hodder Headline

A CIP catalogue record for this title is available from the British Library

ISBN 0 7195 6821 8

Typeset in Monotype Bembo 11.5/15pt by
Palimpsest Book Production Limited, Polmont, Stirlingshire

Printed and bound in Spain by Bookprint S.L., Barcelona

Hodder Headline policy is to use papers that are natural, renewable and recyclable
products and made from wood grown in sustainable forests. The logging and
manufacturing processes are expected to conform to the environmental
regulations of the country of origin.

John Murray (Publishers)
338 Euston Road
London NW1 3BH

Foreword

THE SPACE INVADER, The PR Blonde, The Long Lunchers, The Early Guest, The Brat – most of us have endured all of these Social Stereotypes, and even embodied a few of them (I consider myself more of a PR ashy-brunette). Victoria Mather's gift is for describing these specimens of the human menagerie with alarming acuity and wit, and without a single syllable or detail put wrong. Like Wodehouse and Beerbohm, she's an extrasensory humourist. She has an uncanny ear for the arriviste's aspirational twitticisms and the cranky old codger's internal monologue, and an uncanny eye for the suspiciously wide lapel and the bit of canapé stuck in the teeth. The faux pas, the sly visual joke, the endearing human weakness that speaks volumes to us never fails to be skewered by illustrator extraordinaire Sue Macartney-Snape.

Mather and Macartney-Snape now seem as eternal as Rodgers and Hammerstein, Fortnum & Mason, Noël and Gertie, yet theirs was an arranged marriage. They had only met once before being thrown together by Max Hastings, then editor of the *Daily Telegraph*, to create caricatures of the great and good at the Chelsea Flower Show, that most English of social events. In Notting Hill Macartney-Snape drew fierce dowagers with low-flying bosoms, old brigadiers bent on WMD for slugs and American bankers' wives more aspirant than aspidistra. At the Cannes Film Festival Mather wrote on the back of a couple of envelopes sitting in a bar. Not much has changed. I think they communicate by telepathy as Sue is allergic to answering the telephone (it interrupts Radio 4), has only just mastered e-mail and retreats for months to Australia. Victoria spins round the world as Travel Editor of *Vanity Fair*: this book went in its various stages to Moscow, Mexico and the Maldives. The telephone is useless with her too – it's always the middle of her night. 'Gone snorkelling, do text' was her final communication with her publishers. Yet Social Stereotypes, the column that sprang from Hastings's flower show jaunt to be espoused by Emma Soames for her first edition of the *Telegraph Magazine*, continues through nine time zones. As for Mather's expertise on bars, I can vouchsafe that she introduced me to the best martinis in London, at Duke's Hotel.

I suspect that there are those who gleefully read Mather's vignettes every Saturday and relish Macartney-Snape's subtle visual cruelty, but remain confident that, surely, they could never be summed up so tidily. 'We're too iconoclastic,' they'll say, 'our essences wholly indefinable. That Mather lady may be smart, but she can't touch us.' To which I say read on, suckers – somewhere in this book, you're nailed.

Graydon Carter
New York, 2005

Acknowledgements

After twelve years and 600 Social Stereotypes the question Sue and I are perpetually asked is 'When are you going to run out?' The answer has never been more emphatically 'Never', because never has society danced so fast to the frantic music of the times. Where would we be now without The Celebrity's Girlfriend? The New Tories have a grimly urgent appeal, many of us are closet Mail-Order Addicts, and it was thanks to a School Reunion that I rediscovered remarkable classmates who've achieved great things in the judiciary, medicine, writing and publishing. At the Convent of the Sacred Heart, Woldingham, we were equally inspired and terrified by our headmistress, Mother Clare Shanley – Shan – a legend whose hundredth birthday we celebrated at that reunion, and Mother Dorothy Bell OBE – Ding-Dong, naturally – Mistress of Studies and our geography teacher. Ding-Dong is now 80, frightfully modern, in charge of educational matters in Westminster and co-ordinator for HIV-related work in Southwark diocese. That this is unsurprising is due to my eclectic education at Woldingham, perfect for a nascent journalist's magpie mind, for which I'm eternally gratefully.

The stereotypes herein owe much to many: Annabella Adams, Lis Amherst, Sue Bowen-Jones, Benjamin Clowes, Vernon Colhoun, Daisy Finer, Lucy Fox (so firm on The Bosom), Barry Goodman, John Grandy, Geordie Greig, Clemmie Hambro, Eugenia Korössy, Piers de Laszlo, Sarah Long, Caroline Peel, Andrew Robinson, Anthony Royds, Ann Scott, Andrew Solomon, Sarah Standing, Camilla Swift and Lucia van der Post. Sue's drawing of The Long Lunchers was inspired by the memory of the late and dear Jill Priday who really knew how to enjoy life. The stalwart *Telegraph* team of Vicki Reid, Denis Piggott and Sandie Elsden has kept us on track, while at John Murray Roland Philipps galvanised with lunch at The Wolseley and our editor Caroline Westmore has the patience of a saint. It was nothing to do with a mid-life crisis that my marvellous husband, John Raymond, chose this year to ride his BMW motor bicycle from Moscow to Vladivostok in aid of North Crown Orphanages. It was just courage.

Victoria Mather
London, 2005

Stan and Serry are in denial. There's no such thing as middle age

The Mid-Life Crisis

SERENDIPITY IS HORRIBLY aware that she's entering the environs of the elasticated waistband. Nor do her arms seem long enough to hold pieces of paper 'just up to the light, sweetie' so that she can read them with the naked eye. Stanton won't hear the H-word. 'Hair? Whaddya mean hair? I've plenty of it, but us bikers find the buzzcut is really cool under our Arai helmets. Wanna see my Harley-Davidson?' Born in the Sixties – little Serena became Serendipity when her parents went through the hippy phase – Stan and Serry are in denial. There's no such thing as middle age. It could not possibly happen to them. The fact that Stan now gets meat stuck in his teeth and Serry cannot open any form of packaging is immaterial. She wedges recalcitrant bottles of sesame marinade in the door frame, and when Stan rings his old muckers at their entrepreneurial businesses and is asked to hold on 'because your call is important to us', he throws the telephone out of the window. 'Whatever happened to a real person at the end of the phone?' Serry asks sorrowfully. She is determined to take up yoga so she doesn't get thick ankles. Also to go on the nil-by-mouth diet, learn French and give up drinking. Meanwhile, she'll have another glass. Their daughter, Jasmine, asks with heavy irony whether now is the time for her mother to wear a bra. This is more shocking than Serry's forgetful moment when she put the radio in the fridge and took a litre of milk up to bed. Or the near-erotic excitement inspired by the arrival of rose and bulb catalogues. Fanning herself with *InStyle* – is it frightfully hot, or is it just her? – Serry discounts green tea and HRT. Having wrestled with the wrapping of an OKA delivery (mail order has also crept up on her), she realises that the secret to the meaning of her life now is scissors.

The Dinosaur

SIR MUNGO WAYBACK is bemused by the young thing on his left. Could be rather pretty if she didn't have that savage haircut and such decided opinions. Opinions don't become a woman, particularly on subjects like the euro. Very depressing subject, the euro, it's quite ruined Mungo's holidays in France. Damned Frogs haven't just rounded up, they've tripled everything. Now this young thing – Martha? Mary? – is saying that although doing business in France is complicated, it is the Munich office that is under some pressure. Well, that's damned Huns for you. 'And what business are you in, my dear?' The concept of public relations is difficult for Mungo to grasp, 'public' being unpleasantly associated with transport, and 'relations' with a feral cousin who made his own mantraps and consequently amputated the Waybacks' game-keeper at the knee. Damned inconvenient, good gamekeepers being hard to find. 'So, harrumph, what do you do with this company? Are you a secretary?' Martha replies crisply that she's the managing director, she founded the company, it has an annual turnover of £20 million, and offices in London, Paris, Munich, Milan and 'We've just opened in New York, Sir Mungo, although I am sure you'd hardly credit it since I'm such a ditsy little woman and should be at home bouncing a baby on my knee and cooking rice pudding.'

Rice pudding! Mungo is transported back to the halcyon environs of Nanny, comfort food and the crisp smell of his pyjamas warming on the nursery fireguard. All lost in modern woman's lemming-dash to modernity. He's about to express these regrets to Martha/Mary, together with the bracing story of his survival as a private client stockbroker through several global whoopsies, when he realises he's presented with her furious back.

Sir Mungo thinks opinions don't become a woman

Sally sealed her fate as Sports Day's most embarrassing mother
when she appeared in a hat

The Mother at Sports Day

SALLY HAS WORN trainers so that she can run beside Abigail shouting, 'Faster, darling, faster! Mummy's here' in the three-legged race. She has thus sealed her fate as the day's most embarrassing mother, having been odds-on favourite from the moment she appeared in a hat. 'Mum, that's so gross,' hisses Abigail, mortified. Her friends' mothers are in backless Tod's, and haven't confused this summer's hippy-dippy look with a dirndl skirt bought from a stall at Devon County Show. Nor is the Sound of Music waistcoat good. Then there's the picnic. Her friends' mothers at St Mary's all have teak garden furniture disgorged from the back of Range Rovers, and wine, and smoked salmon and coronation chicken – 'It's so retro, the Cath Kidston of food' – and packet salad from M&S. But Sally has a Toyota, holey rug, lemonade, homemade cheese sandwiches and wonky tomatoes from Dad's Grobag. The pièce de résistance is the disposable barbecue which leaves a horrid burn mark on the velvet sward of the hockey pitch. Abigail is going to die. When she does the long jump Dad takes pictures of the wrong girl because he's so short-sighted. Abigail hopes she is adopted, and that one day it will be discovered that she is the long-lost daughter of a Russian prince. Sally greets her every little effort with rapturous enthusiasm: 'Darling, you're such a little competitor. Mrs Fanshawe, isn't Abigail such a joiner-inner? I'm sure she should have this year's prize for trying.' Abigail knows she's pathetic at games, she'd rather be reading Jacqueline Wilson, or have Daisy Armitage's mother as a mother. Mrs Armitage is beauty editor on *Gloss* and won't allow Daisy to play hockey in case she gets thick legs. As Sally puffs around beside Abigail, bosom a flopping spinnaker, Abigail stops dead like Devon Loch and bursts into tears.

The English Tourist in Australia

ZOE DOESN'T KNOW which she finds more irritating – the flies or the natives. She came to Australia to get a tan, didn't she? To get really fit. To toast away pimply grey skin in the blinding light of the southern hemisphere. Yet every time she ventures out into the sun in dear little strappy dresses exposing her pale English limbs, people rush at her with suncreams, the strength of which could block out a nuclear explosion. They ask sadly how can she drink alcohol in the sun. It's so bad for her. But Zoe smiles beatifically and says that seems a terrible shame when Australian wine is so delicious. A top drop. Aussie hunks insist that she wears a hat. What sissy behaviour is this? Zoe thought the Oz culture was all about beer, brawn and Bruces who surfed Bondi on the backs of Great White Sharks. Not saddos droning on about the hole in the ozone layer and slip-slap-slop. 'It's what we're taught in life-saving classes now, Zoe, slip on a shirt, slap on a hat, slop on some suncream,' but Zoe thinks factor 60 would stain her Dolce & Gabbana shirt dreadfully.

Willowy women who are obviously offshoots of Elle McPherson are negotiating the sand dunes in full-length clothing; whither the bikini? A facial beak, prophylactic against a red-nose day, appears to be a bisexual accessory, and all children are encased in Day-Glo neoprene sunsuits lest they contract cancer while building sandcastles. Zoe, who had looked forward to the untrammelled joys of sun and fun, to barbies at which she could wear little bits of clothing tied together with string, is dazed and confused. She came for a bronze-up, she's got an eco-lecture, and what the hell is she supposed to do about the damned flies? Frightfully sorry, bloody blowies.

Zoe came to Oz for a bronze-up and has got an eco-lecture

Will this make me look big on T.V.? A Question For our time

COFFER

A UNIQUE AND ABSOLUTELY FASCINATING OBLIQUE VIEW OF HISTORY FROM AN ANGLE NOONE'S EVER THOUGHT OF BEFORE BY ME

ANOTHER UNIQUE & TERRIBLY INTELLIGENT TOME by ME

Damien's speciality is historical icons with exciting sex lives

The Trendy Historian

DAMIEN IS INORDINATELY pleased with his new book, *Vlad the Plod: The Glutton, the Sadist, the Comic*. Slavic history will never be the same again; forget Peter Mandelson, Vladimir is going to be the new prince of darkness. Publication is exquisitely timed to coincide with his new Channel 4 series on Carthage, in which he is dressed in a Ralph Lauren Polo shirt and chinos and says repeatedly to camera, 'Rome was Carthage's worst nightmare', while standing on old ruins. Damien likes a ravaged civilisation, they illustrate the cyclical imperative of history or 'What goes around, comes around' – confiding look to camera, tanned arm out-thrown towards Vesuvius. He thought his deconstruction of Pompeii went awfully well; after all, he read Pliny in the original and his old tutor at Oxford was delightfully complimentary. Damien is anticipating sitting on top table at his next gaudy. Of course it has been frustrating that Sebag has bagged Stalin – but really, could one have been bothered to learn Russian and eat cabbage soup for a year in Moscow? – and Adam Zamoyski's *Napoleon* had marvellous illustrations, but Napoleon's been rather done, doesn't one think?

What Damien desires is a fascinating historical icon who preferably spent his formative years in Monte Carlo and went on to conquer several East European capitals in which there are now Four Seasons hotels. Budapest, Prague, Istanbul; all would be charming places in which to spend a little time, and so televisual. The historical icon should also have had an exciting sex life, preferably with one or some of the following: Catherine the Great, Marie Antoinette, Lucretia Borgia, several Medicis and Margaret Thatcher. Not that he approves of modern history, it's far too easy for others to check his sources on the internet.

The Bosom

THE BOSOM PRECEDES Dymphna up staircases and into drawing-rooms. It is not a phenomenon to be asked to an intimate supper in a bedsit, since other guests might be pillowed against the wall. A not unpleasurable experience, which is why Dymphna is a popular guest and has long since ceased to struggle with the fact that she is the supporting cast to a social continental shelf. There was a moment in her twenties, when she was constantly teased about toppling over on the pavement – 'Miracle how you stand upright, my fine beauty' – that she thought about breast reduction, but bras like slingshots from Rigby & Peller gave her Madonna-appeal.

Dymphna dresses according to her assets. The result is an independent structure that is Richard Rogers meets Nigella: an architectural expression of womanly supremacy. Wrestling the bosom into jackets is a challenge, ditto cashmere sweaters, which has the two-puppies-in-a-sack effect, but Dymphna has opted for rest-your-head-here appeal and many have thought this delightful, albeit with a snorkel as precaution against being smothered. By remaining aloof from her embonpoint, she implies that she lives on a separate planet, floating high above the main concourse of her body, which could have shopping malls and jumbo jet aircraft attached. Actually, Dymphna lives with two other people jumbling around her frontage; forget spaghetti straps, she requires road haulage. When she tried an Armani suit it ended up under her armpits; a Marks & Sparks lacy bra is so voluminous she could sail across the world trouncing Ellen MacArthur. Shirts gape; the bikini top is wobbling blancmange zone. Sometimes Dymphna feels she's about to explode.

Dymphna has opted for rest-your-head-here appeal

At the bar lunch flows into the late afternoon.
It then seems pointless going home

The Arts Club

IT IS COCKTAIL hour at the Arts Club, but then it always is. Evangeline tottered in at noon, having written a savage article on German Expressionism, and has been in pole position at the bar since lunch flowed into the late afternoon. It then seemed pointless going home. Fortescue Maynard, who sculpts, has now awoken from his siesta in an ancient wing chair and is testing the club's new consignment of claret. Deirdre, in need of revival after an exhausting couple of hours modelling nude at the Slade, is ably assisting this research. By the third glass she's excoriating the *Daily Mail* for being fatist and Fascist, only it's proving quite difficult to say. Despising the *Mail* is a favourite Arts Club pastime; critics are also spawn of the devil who know nothing, with the exception of Brian Sewell who is currently in favour with Evangeline, and Rod the barman, for having declared the Brit Art fire one of the happiest days of his life. It is mandatory to hate Tracey Emin and Damien Hirst because they're frightfully successful and rich. Charles Saatchi has never bought anything from an Arts Club member, not even from the more alternative ones who wear Birkenstocks and smoke cigarillos.

Rod, after one of his Pernod sessions, once grouped the club's overflowing ashtrays together as an installation called *Holocaust*, but people kept flicking their ash in it. Evangeline, when infuriated by writer's block and Chardonnay, is known to stub Marlboro Lights out in the club's excellent fish pie. Then chef knows they're in for a bumpy night; the time Vange put hot chips down Fortescue's collar when he voted to admit antique dealers as members is remembered affectionately. All the Arts Club regulars go on little regimes when they say they'll just have one drink; fortunately the glasses are as big as vases.

The Tennis Coach

GREG IS QUITE the favourite of the yummy mummies at the Ritzdale Club. There is Adrian, but he always gets a bit too close when demonstrating the correct serve action, standing behind Amanda Wyldbore to swish her racket arm to and fro. Greg is more bracing, less blandishments. He makes the mummies feel safe, and Patsy Pringle says they need a teacher, not a sex object. (Amanda isn't so sure.)

Greg is thus much in demand by these terrifyingly fit women, who bounce into the club straight from taking their children to extra Japanese tuition. At least, that is what Patsy is making Petunia Pringle do this holidays; Amanda is reluctant to admit that her son requires extra RI tuition. 'My dear Amanda, a domestic pet could pass the GCSE in religious instruction,' says Patsy as they knock up. Greg is most encouraged that Amanda subsequently plays with considerable aggression. He gives her an encouraging pat on the shoulder, and Amanda feels quite overcome with gratitude and also notices what terrific legs Greg has, elegant, like a tanned giraffe. The father figure is definitely better than the sex object. Greg is fit – no paunch, unlike her flabby husband – and you have to be a real man or a colonial governor to look authoritative in shorts. Greg is definitely a love. 'He qualified for Wimbledon, Patsy, he's played tennis since he was three.' Patsy says it's people like that who think they're good, then get into the shark pool with the really good, and realise they're never going to be good enough. With which Greg would good-naturedly concur. Yet he's made a healthy life, has a pretty house on the river and a Joan Hunter Dunn wife, all from giving others confidence about the game that's his passion.

Only real men or colonial governors look good in shorts

Is three hours going to be enough time for check-in?

The Bad Traveller

KATIE WOKE AT three in the morning, beset with anxiety about missing her plane at noon. Had she really booked the taxi? Was an hour going to be enough for the journey to Heathrow, given the morning rush? Was three hours going to be enough for check-in, with the new security procedures? Would the boarding gate be number 156, thus requiring a walk of 25 minutes with huge amounts of awesomely heavy hand luggage? Katie often wonders whatever happened to gate number one. By 3.30am she has got up to re-pack her suitcases, because after all one doesn't know about the weather, and Nanny always said to take a jumper, and one can never have too many white T-shirts, and she can't remember where she's put the Imodium. That Katie is only travelling to France is irrelevant to this panic attack. The Dordogne is notorious for dodgy weather, and it would certainly be unwise to trust foie gras-induced dyspepsia to the local pharmacist. Katie knows enough to realise that the French cure-all is the suppository.

Arriving at check-in before the flight even *has* a check-in, she can't find her passport. Was it in her handbag, or the travel case slung around her neck for extra security among thieving foreigners? Or did she leave it in the taxi, on the hall table, or – a favourite hiding-place for slippery valuables – the dog basket? Oops, here it is in her pocket. Katie is now pink with effort, the dew of sweat on her upper lip. The boarding pass evaporates to the planet for lost bits of paper before she gets to departures. Then there's the credit card payment she has to post in case she dies in-flight, only she hasn't a stamp. Finally pinned in her budget airline seat, Katie thinks of the bliss of staying at home.

The New Tories

ED IS IN advertising. Of course he knows Maurice Saatchi; Maurice is his guru. Of course he knows David Cameron; they were at Oxford together. Of course he knows Rachel Whetstone; she was at Benenden with his wife, Rose. Rose was in the Conservative Research Department, now she has a newspaper column, marvellously well-cut hair, and the 'I-got-a-first-and-I-also-have-a-cleavage' arrogance that upstages 4x4 mothers at the Little Genius Kindergarten. Rose always walks her children to school herself because she believes in parental responsibility, the lack of which, as she has frequently written, is the source of social breakdown under New Labour. Her political sensibilities have been outraged by police taxiing teenage tearaways from some sink estate to St Dunce's because their single mothers can't be bothered to get out of bed. It's these idle Sharons painting their toes while watching *Richard & Judy* who force Ed and Rose to employ an extra illegal Filipina to nanny their children in the Notting Hill communal garden. Who knows what recidivist youth might leap over the railings to steal their Playmobil? At dinner at Zucca the other night – in between Euroscepticism and the risotto – Ed said to Boris that a harsh anti-crime initiative had to be a key component of the Tory war-footing offensive. Boris nodded his hair vigorously and thought he'd just pop out and check he'd put the chain on his bicycle.

Rose, an avid tax-cutter, is writing her next column on how staff should be deductible, ditto gym memberships to reduce the nation's obesity problem. 'I've told George Osborne that the politics of the Spoilt Society has to be draconian: hand-chopping-offing for litter louts, chewing-gum tax, dog-poo police armed with machine guns, and those fraudsters who ring up old ladies and tell them they've won a million pounds must be castrated.'

Ed is in advertising; Rose has a newspaper column.
They know everybody

*Nothing she is wearing belongs to her,
including much of her body*

The Celebrity's Girlfriend

HAYLEY STOBBS WAS once glimpsed in *Hollyoaks*. She has an upcoming nanosecond as a road-accident victim in *Holby City*, but is on the cusp of celebrity by virtue of being Ryan Ferret's girlfriend. Ryan is up for the People's Award as Best-Looking Newcomer. Hayley is up for anything: interviews in *Heat* magazine, sharing her beauty tips with Trinny, modelling in *OK!* Nothing she is wearing on the red carpet actually belongs to her, including much of her body. There's the nose job, the breast enhancement and significant engineering work on her teeth. She's had her bottom buffed so that, despite freezing temperatures, it will glow like twin Cox's Orange Pippins. Jodie from Screen Slap make-up has Polyfilla'd every minuscule acne pit, applied eyelashes individually with Stick-It, enhanced lips with Plump-Up, and no crevice remains unwaxed. Gary at Top Knotch has put so much product in Hayley's hair extensions that the effect is of sculpted cardboard, slightly as if Jessica Rabbit had come to life. Now it is showtime.

Hayley puts her pedicured feet forward and wiggles for the cameras in her Jimmy Choos. The cold makes essential parts of her quite pert. 'This way, love! Give us a flash, Hayley! Whoa, Ryan, tomorrow everyone's gonna be saying, "Who's that guy with Hayley Stobbs?"' Move over Liz Hurley, forget Versace and his safety pins, Sputnik's dress in spandex chiffonette is doing it for her. Make love to the camera, baby, and next thing you'll be the face of Lancôme, the spirit of Chanel No 5, the star of *Strictly Come Dancing*. During the walk of fame anything seems possible. She's up there, saying, 'Hey, Jude, Hi, Sienna.' She's a contender, not just Ryan's babe, until the Cinderella moment when she puts her borrowed bling back in its box.

'Who does most of the driving, sir? Are we a one-car family?'

The Car Buyers

IT TOOK ANNE two minutes to establish the car's essential details: its colour, where the cup-holder is for her Starbucks' cappuccino, and whether she could get Radio 4 by pressing a button marked '4'. Nothing else is of any interest to her. Meanwhile, Mark is talking the torque with Mr Sprockit, and they've warmed up into grunt and poke, as in 'This car's got the poke to get you out of trouble, sir.' Anne wonders if Mr Sprockit will be coming home to have lunch with them, or perhaps to spend the night, so that he can fully elaborate on the engine's grunting capabilities, not to mention the joys of the individually controlled air-conditioning systems. Anne can just summon a batsqueak of interest in this, as it will be marvellous for the dog to be iced down. Previously she's had to travel in a fur coat in July with the air-con on max throughout so that Wolfgang doesn't expire. Separate climatic zones will be perfect provided Mark isn't in the car as well. Whenever Anne attempts to adjust the controls, he gets St Vitus-twitchy, batting her hand out of the way, saying 'Don't do that, you don't understand it.' Or, even more irritating, 'You don't need to be any warmer.' As if need had anything to do with it.

Mr Sprockit is now confiding the dazzling intricacies of the satellite navigation system, which consists of a Lady Thatcher voice in the dashboard telling one to go right at the next exit, which one could perfectly well have deduced from the signpost. But Mark's eyes glitter, and Mr Sprockit asks about their lifestyle. 'Who does most of the driving, sir? Are we a one-car family? Do we have any little people still at school? Do we ski? Allow me to show you the Zumo Dingbat's special modification for transporting skis.' Anne's lip curls savagely; she's in an edition of *Top Gear* and Mark has turned into Jeremy Clarkson.

'Show me the Monet!' is his little joke when confronted with a dubious picture

The Antiques Expert

HUGH HAS FOUND his *métier*. His phantasmagoric bow ties are perfectly suited to television; he is the Robin Day of the porcelain figurine, exuding an unctuous enthusiasm ripe for the daytime slot of *Antiques Workshop*. Middle-aged women with crisp hair are so dazzled as to be unaware that his hand-fluttering delight over Great-Aunt Maud's mourning brooch is exquisitely patronising, curdled with the milk of human kindness. 'My good lady, what a story this trinket tells. I detect real human hair within the crystal – could dear, dear Aunt Maud have suffered a deceased child? A blond infant untimely snatched from her by the whooping cough? Woe is me to contemplate her loss. Ah! A Wemyss pig! My dear sir, did you know that the Prince of Wales himself is a great fancier of Wemyss pigs?' Hugh is obtuse about actual monetary value – 'To you, my friend, the sentimental value must be immense. This is what matters, not filthy lucre' – while having negotiated a fat contract for himself from PopKulture Productions.

His professional bonhomie is notably lacking in the dressing-room, where the producer is treated to a hissy fit about Hong Kong tat being brought to him as Ming vases. Hugh is as keen as anyone to discover a masterpiece. 'Show me the Monet!' is his little joke when confronted with a dubious picture hauled out of an attic. He dreams of the newspaper stories when a six-figure sum is realised at auction for 'a discovery by Hugh de Bonville', that was used as a cat-litter tray in a provincial hovel before his expert eye winkled it out. After a day gushing over horrors from the Franklin Mint, Hugh thinks soothing thoughts of the decorative arts of the 1930s. What he would give to find a silver-leaf Italian shell-settee. This *tendre* for flamboyance is why Hugh's colleagues at Christoby's are delighted he's away so much.

The Competitive Grannies

GRANNY SYBIL SAYS that Joshua should be in bed by six o'clock, lights out and no nonsense. Granny Annie says why on earth shouldn't the poor little mite stay up until he feels like going to bed, all the children on the continent do. Granny Sybil, who likes to be called Granny, opines that this is precisely why foreigners are so undisciplined and volatile. Granny Annie, who likes to be called Annie, gives Josh a consoling drink of Coca-Cola when Granny Sybil isn't looking. Sybil is against fizzy drinks – 'Nothing wrong with God's own water' – which, together with crisps, sweets and eating between meals, are the unfortunate leitmotifs of the council-estate child. Annie has a shockingly lax attitude to demand feeding, and is incapable of passing the ice-cream van in the park without buying a whipped cornet with two Cadbury's flakes. On Joshua's birthday she took him to the Wolseley for tea and they ate everything backwards, starting with a *coup de glace*, progressing to cake, then egg sandwiches. Granny Sybil, who thinks eating cake before bread and butter instils criminal tendencies, counter-attacked with a visit to her local country-house hotel. Her daughter-in-law was instructed to dress Joshua in his sailor suit and Joshua was made to sit up straight, and eat wholemeal toast and carrot sticks in a whispery dining room. He wasn't allowed to play on the lawn in case he got grass stains.

The grannies have been firmly separated for the bucket-and-spade holiday in Cornwall. Granny Annie will arrive with a blow-up rubber whale and a bottle of gin; Granny Sybil will arrive with insect repellent and her own sheets. If the sun is too strong she'll make everyone stay indoors playing improving games from the Early Learning Centre. The exquisite tension of granny wars may preclude Joshua from ever having siblings.

*Granny Annie buys ice cream; Granny Sybil thinks
bad eating habits instil criminal tendencies*

The Sales Shopper

FRAN IS IN a state of orgiastic excitement. She does not need a puce chiffon cocktail frock lined in lurid citrus sateen, but at £850, reduced from a near-as-dammit £2,000, it's a steal. The wrong size, but it can always be taken in. It won't be, of course. This putrid garment will fester in the back of Fran's cupboard together with other sales mistakes: the trousers that need taking up, the jacket that could easily be Chanel if the buttons were changed, the skirt that will fit perfectly when she loses weight. It is a reproachful collection, but now, in the thrill of the chase, Fran is indulging in free shopping. For someone virtually innumerate, the accuracy with which she remembers her pin numbers is astonishing. It's hardly like spending money at all. There will be a very depressing day in February when the credit card bills hit the mat, and she'll require a massive vodka and tonic to get over the incomprehensible cost of saving so much money. But it's nothing a trip to Zara to cheer herself up won't put right.

Meanwhile, Fran deploys the serpentine cunning of a guerrilla warrior circumnavigating revolting rails of surplus stock in Debenhams, all the while dodging Ultrabrite young women attempting to sell her store cards. She's much too sales-savvy to go anywhere near the wonderful worlds of electronics, where over-weight men will be bargaining about plasma screens. Anything practical doesn't seem like fun at all, although she did once buy a juicer, intending to pulverise carrots and cabbage into healthy and palatable form. Strangely, it's never been out of its box. Long, long ago she lost the instructions for the ice-cream maker, bought in a perfect hostess fantasy moment in Harrods. Now she's piling the carrier bags into her Audi A3. They'll be removed under cover of darkness while her husband is watching *Newsnight*.

The cost of saving so much money is incomprehensible

The Dropper-In

WHEN THE DOORBELL clangs deep in the heart of the Old
Rectory, Miles and Claire look at each other appalled. Surely not
the gasman coming to read the meter on a Saturday? Perhaps Mrs
Gilpin with her petition about saving the village post office? Or a
burglar checking whether they are in? When they cautiously open
the front door, there is Elaine. 'Coo-ee! I was just passing, and
thought I'd drop in on the off-chance. Dying to see your new
house. You don't mind, do you?' Miles and Claire mind very much,
but it's too late. Elaine is already in the hall – 'Are these flagstones
original?' – handing Miles her coat. Claire furiously wonders how
Elaine, who was their neighbour in Clapham, could possibly be just
passing in Dorset. 'Claire, I can bring the dachsie in, can't I? You
remember Banger.' Claire indeed remembers Banger as a flatulent
hairbrush who yapped horribly at her Siamese. She weakly fills the
kettle. 'An Aga, Claire. How marvellous, although it's a shame it's
cream. It shows the dirt so. But probably you'll be taking it out
when you redo the kitchen?' Miles replies tartly that they have just
redone the kitchen, that the subtle arts of Mr Farrow and Mr Ball
have been deployed at some expense to make it look as if it has
always been like this.

Claire scrabbles for Rich Tea biscuits, last deployed for nice Mr
Waters, the plumber. As Elaine rabbits on about travelling down for
her Aunt Violet's 80th birthday in Piddletrenthide, both Miles and
Claire stand as if about to go somewhere. Claire is aware that the
clock is ticking up to lunchtime. Elaine sits firm. 'Er, do stay, only
got pasta, missed the organic farm shop now. Miles will show you
the drawing room, where *Sense and Sensibility* was filmed. Won't
you, Miles?' In doing so, he steps in a poo Banger has deposited on
the Aubusson.

'I was just passing and thought I'd drop in on the off-chance'

Mr Liversedge has no truck with the euphemism

The Harley Street Specialist

MR LIVERSEDGE IS full of good cheer about growths and tumours. For him, a really satisfactory exploratory procedure is one that promises a complex challenge to his skills on the operating table. Given a potentially terminal condition, Mr Liversedge's bedside manner is so bracing that the patient, woozy from the anaesthetic, feels blessed to be providing the specialist with such an interesting voyage around their insides. 'There's so much we can do nowadays,' Mr Liversedge beams, flapping milky-white hands, his gold signet ring and cufflinks flashing. He glows with health and prosperity, his pinstripe suit (stripes a little too wide) is bespoke, his brogues by Lobb's.

Fizzing with energy, he makes his ward rounds about 6.30am, again when the patients are somewhat weak and bemused and won't waste his time asking questions. Much better not, as Mr Liversedge has no truck with the euphemism and does not refer to massed cells when he means a lump. Only after he has vanished in a crowd of acolytes do they realise that they know nothing about their medical progress and everything about Mr Liversedge's day at Ascot and forthcoming weekend at his house in the south of France. Many feel better for this. Things can't be all bad if Liversedge is on the champagne run, eh? The National Health patients don't know or care about Mr Liversedge's merry expectations of lunch at La Voile D'Or, but know enough to feel patronised. They would certainly not care for his driver, his 7-series BMW or his Georgian house in Hampshire, even though the prosperity these manifest enables him to work in the state sector. On Fridays he always wears a bow tie. 'An Hermès tie gets dreadfully in the way when I'm doing haemorrhoid operations.'

The Consort

ELIZA IS PERPETUALLY someone's wife or someone's girlfriend, which requires iron discipline, cosmetic surgery and an eerie wardrobe. On the merry-go-round of lucrative divorce settlements she cannot afford to let anything slip, certainly not her chin. She is obsessively co-ordinated, a look taken to an extreme that makes her resemble an airmail envelope. A look so scarily Nancy Reagan it shrieks 'Don't touch', which is curious for someone who has devoted her life to men. Born in Reading, although she refers vaguely to a childhood in Henley, Eliza first married Doug, who was 20 years older, owned a brick factory and died of a massive heart attack, leaving her all his money. Eliza has very fond memories of Doug. She bought a house in Chelsea, did some light modelling and met Jeremy. He was a Porsche-driving, perma-tanned habitué of the Med. They had a lot of fun on a lot of yachts but when she found him in bed with a cabin boy Eliza left Jeremy, taking a substantial sum from his father for purposes of discretion.

It was at the Chelsea Flower Show gala preview that she met Sir Malcolm Lavishe, head of Gush Oil. A widower, he obviously needed her. She ran his houses in London, Wiltshire and Lyford Cay immaculately; she saw that he always had his favourite food, even though it meant she endured five years of roast lamb. But it hardly matters when one doesn't eat. Their parties were perfect down to the last white parrot tulip. Eliza murmured flattering nothings to city titans; the scent of power has always been the most heady to her. After Malcolm's stroke she had her eyes done, and decided she deserved an Italian industrialist. There have been two more marriages but Eliza has resolutely continued to call herself Lady Lavishe.

The merry-go-round of lucrative divorce settlements
requires iron discipline and cosmetic surgery

Holly chants, 'My mother's a loser', as Amanda stutters around the birds and the bees

The Chat About the Facts of Life

AMANDA HAS DECIDED to tackle this thorny subject while in the car on the way back to school. She has told herself that this is so Holly cannot escape, but actually it is because she, Amanda, has failed to seize the moment during the exeat. The intended cosy chat over the Aga was negated by the mordant fear of Holly walking out of the kitchen saying 'Puh-leeeze'. Now, at 80mph, she begins, 'Darling, I think we have to have a little talk . . .' Only for Holly to put her fingers in her ears, while simultaneously shouting, 'My mother's a loser, my mother's a loser', to block out the humiliation of Amanda's stuttering tiptoe around the birds and the bees. Every time Holly takes her fingers out of her ears, to check if the torture is over, she hears gross things like, 'When two people really love each other', and 'Your father and I'. Yuck, that is so pants. How could these ghastly old people ever have sex? Amanda is now scarlet in the face, fumbling her way towards condoms and sexually transmitted diseases.

It's way too much information, and a battle ensues with the CD player, Holly turning up Robbie Williams to blast out her mother's pathetic medical details, and Amanda punching him off, saying, 'Let's be adult about this, Holly.' Both are exceedingly cross. 'Mum, I know it all. It's total tongue sandwiches at the Feathers Ball and everyone snogs on Daymer Beach.' Amanda's suspicions about these two inevitabilities are confirmed. In one hideous moment passing Basingstoke, Rock becomes a shagathon. She's never going to allow Holly to go again. Holly punishes her mother with details of dogging, which has nothing to do with their Labrador. For once, both are infinitely relieved to get back to school.

The Archaeologist

RHODA WANTED TO be an archaeologist from the moment she and her father found a Roman coin in the garden at Badgecourt, their Gunpowder Plot house. She was eight, all her contemporaries were in pink ballet shoes being Sugar Plum fairies at Miss Baverstock's music and movement classes in the village hall, but Rhoda preferred grubbing in the earth. Treasure was supposed to be buried at the house to finance the gunpowder plotters and Rhoda and her father set out to find it. A futile search, but one which gave them both enormous pleasure, with the anticipation of secret passages, priest's holes and swag. Cook said furiously that their priest's hole was a baking oven and would they please get out of her kitchen.

Nothing gave Rhoda's father greater pleasure than her place at Oxford to read archaeology; next stop would surely be a Tutankhamun's tomb. Yet Rhoda has been entirely happy with the painstaking, minuscule work of earth-shifting with a toothbrush, usually in fierce climates aerated only by the whiff of camel dung. It would be marvellous to excavate a naive clay bull with an acrobat holding one horn (as seen in the Archaeological Museum of Iraklion on Crete), or an early example of Kamaresware pottery with polychrome decoration, but Rhoda never aspired to a eureka moment unearthing a Babylonian Processional Street, dating from King Nebuchadnezzar. She is content with the pot-washers of ancient history, the detritus of domestic life. She did once find an amphora from the Cretan New-Palace age, a wine vessel decorated with octopus. How she imagined the party. Oblivious to sunscreen, a stranger to the looking glass, shoulders strong from pushing wheelbarrows of earth, Rhoda's romantic ambition would be to find another Roman coin.

*Rhoda's painstaking work is in fierce climates aerated
by the whiff of camel dung*

The Beach Wedding

BRIAN AND SHELLEY wanted it just to be them, alone in a tropical paradise, the waves lapping and sand between their toes. Unfortunately the beaches in Mauritius are all public, so the wedding photographs will reveal a motley crowd of sarong sellers and pot-bellied tourists gathered interestedly at the water's edge. Also, one of those local winds that drives peasants mad has whipped up to threaten the hibiscus arch, centrepiece of the Hearts and Flowers package at the Hotel Romantica. (Each evening in the Passion Suite with balcony and sea view, the maid outlines a heart on their bed in bougainvillaea petals, which get uncomfortably entwined in Shelley's nightie from Brides of Surrey.) A beaming official, stiff with gold braid, conducts a ceremony punctuated by a Beach Boys CD. Brian is a surfin' flower-power remnant. The Romantica's general manager, crisp in a suit and tie decorated with palm trees, reprises his regular role as chief witness. Brian wanted his son to come but Dylan said Arsenal were playing; Shelley's daughter removed her iPod from her ears long enough to mutter that she wasn't sitting on a beach with Beardie Brian. Fortunately the in-law problem has been sorted by the Grim Reaper.

So here are Brian and Shelley having their hey-man kaftan moment among total strangers. Brian has had the Bridegrooming Facial (tricky with the beard) and a back-wax; Shelley settled blushingly for the aphrodisiac massage with essential oils. She fell asleep. After the ceremony they will paddle hand in hand in the water, while the photographer runs backwards in front of them shouting, in the teeth of the wind, 'Smile, Shellee, be very happy peoples, please.' And they are. After vile years married to a disagreeable solicitor, Shelley's second husband is her yoga teacher.

*Brian and Shelley are having their hey-man kaftan moment
among total strangers*

The Long-Suffering Accountant

MR FUDGITT IS sadly bemused by Claudia. Money and figures are colour and light to him, the reassuring logic of life's order, yet here is this delightful creature who is financially incontinent. It seems unnatural. Claudia's visits to Mr Fudgitt are heralded by breathy telephone calls saying that she's got in a bit of a muddle, and 'can it really be time for that horrid VAT again, Mr Fudgitt?' Her progress up the stairs to Mr Fudgitt's office on the first floor of Phibbs and Fudgitt is marked by a paper trail of old taxi receipts. He had just been working on the accounts of a blissfully dull engineering company, now his reproduction mahogany desk is covered with overflowing carrier bags. 'You told me to save all my bills, Mr Fudgitt,' Claudia says triumphantly, before going into a state of shock, from which he has to resuscitate her with tea, about the amount of the VAT, not to mention her tax due on January 31. 'There must be a mistake, Mr Fudgitt, I don't think I've even earned that much. It's a fortune and I never have any money, so I can't possibly owe it in silly old VAT, can I?' Mr Fudgitt presses his fingertips together in a little cathedral of supplication and utters soothing advice about tax allowances and reclaiming VAT. 'Many of your expenses, like, er, pencils and paints and perhaps graph paper? As you're a graphic artist, let's call them materials. They have VAT on them, which you can reclaim if you file the receipts.' They both then gaze in silent wonder at the plastic repositories of Claudia's filing system. Claudia flutters her elegantly helpless artist's hands, and Mr Fudgitt takes the line of least resistance: 'I tell you what, my dear, leave it all to me.'

'You told me to save all my bills,'
Claudia says triumphantly

'Why', Maurice wonders, 'is everyone in such a tearing hurry?'

The Ancient Driver

MAURICE IS NOW so hunched over the wheel that the car looks as if it is driving itself. This ghostly vision trundling down the centre of the road is enhanced by the wisps of smoke emitting from the passenger window. Peggy, a dab of purple rinse barely visible above the dashboard, is a great one for a ciggie in the car. It calms her nerves, other drivers these days being so perfectly frightful. No manners, fiends the lot of them, particularly the women in those truck things. The hooting is unforgivable when one of them gets stuck behind Maurice as he carefully and slowly makes his way along the white line. He has even had to endure some exceedingly vulgar language at the traffic lights. It is fortunate that Maurice is partially deaf, so that the adjective qualifying 'old geezer' passes him by. A pleasant outing to Waitrose could otherwise become upsetting.

Why, Maurice wonders, is everyone in such a tearing hurry? It's the same when he and Peggy go to the Plume of Feathers at Stoke Widdle. They do a very good steak and kidney pie at luncheon, but a gentle drive through the country lanes at 30mph is impaired by the steaming queue of traffic that builds up behind him. The other day a man in a BMW actually shook his fist at Maurice, but what can you expect from a fellow in a German car with his jacket hung on a little hook? It's the flashers who upset Maurice, driving up his bottom flicking their lights. Downright dangerous – what if he were to brake? Which he frequently does so a dear little partridge can make its leisurely way across the road. They mate for life – Maurice doesn't want to make an avian widow. As he chunters through the village, putting out his indicator at least 200 yards before the pub, the vicar remarks, 'There goes the Maurice Minor.'

The Early Guest

POLLY WRENCHES THE Carmens out of her hair on the helter-skelter down the stairs when the doorbell rings. Ohmigod. Simon is still in the bath. They'd definitely said 8.30, and that it was not smart, but here is Celine shimmering on the doorstep with the superiority of one who has been to the hairdresser, had a manicure and languorous hours in which to choose from myriad cashmere fashion statements. She raises one waxed eyebrow as much as is possible with Botox, eyes Polly, who is frantically clutching her Mason Pearson and a broken sandal, and says, 'I'm not early, am I?' Polly gallantly pops a smile on, squeaking, 'No, no, not early a bit, everyone else late, wonderful to see you, glass of champagne?' and is horribly aware that her face is greasy with sweat from bending over the oven for the past four hours.

Until Simon emerges, pink and scrubbed, to hold the fort, she is stuck making tiny talk with Celine while dinner burns. Celine is not the sort of person who can be left alone with the *Evening Standard*. Celine wants to be entertained – which means telling Polly about how she's off to New York to shop 'Because with the two-dollar pound one really can't afford not to', and that Polly's house is remarkably easy to get to, despite being south of the river. Polly is saved by the doorbell. Flinging the other guests at Celine she manages a hectic flight upstairs to blot her face, scrabble for a lipstick and hiss at Simon – 'It's Celine, and she's your bloody friend' – before the mercy dash to the kitchen where the potatoes have boiled dry. It is surely never like this for Nigella. Celine can be heard trilling about how New York friends always give dinner for her in restaurants. A thunderous clatter and filthy swearing indicate that Simon has slipped on a Carmen roller on the stairs.

'I'm not early, am I?'

This England. All being buggered by Blair

The Lawn Meet

THE MASTER LIKES having the lawn meet at Pockley Court; marvellously long drive so the police can cut the antis off at the park gates. The Cheesbroughs bought Pockley only a couple of years ago, he's some banker thingy, but Flick Cheesbrough is trying awfully hard to fit into country life, so she produces food way over the top, which everyone, having stuffed themselves, can criticise when hanging around hunting 'legally'. Dick Cheesbrough may smile too much – hence 'Cheesy' Cheesbrough – but he makes a damn good electric soup, thermoses of boiling vodka thinly disguised with consommé, plus fine port enhanced with presentation by Jemma Cheesbrough, whom the Master's son tells him is a fit chick. Flick, thinking that 7lb of cocktail sausages and 60 miniature pork pies might not be enough, did a mercy run to Marks & Spencer and bought their entire stock of breadcrumbed goujons of sole. Meg, who comes and helps everyone with their drinks parties (so her presence with the Cheesbroughs means they're accepted), has thrust these in the Aga, plus oven chips, and is handing them round with ketchup, firmly jabbing swivelling horses' rumps with her elbow.

The field is so enormous that the sausages have almost gone; those who took up hunting as a protest against their civil liberties being interfered with have realised they missed out on a lifelong drinks party. The Master feels sentiment curdled with Taylor's Vintage. This glorious meadow, ducks in the river, the mellow William and Mary house, the pale sun on the frosty fingers of the trees. This England. All being buggered by Blair. The huntsman sounds his horn in the crisp air, and the Master leads off as if it is the last cavalry charge. They have a splendid time and the whipper-in says it was the best fish and chips he ever had.

Of course Cornelia doesn't need a blackamoor candelabra,
but he was so seductive

The Magpie

CORNELIA ONCE BROUGHT a piano home on Eurostar. She'd found it in a Paris flea market, divinely painted but challenging to transport, even in first class. Cornelia has never been defeated by logistics. There were the shells, gathered on an Australian beach, which she wrapped in loo paper and took as hand luggage in a cold box. No one told her it was illegal. She'd just have said, 'Oh really, darling? But they'll look so pretty in my bathroom.' The white heat of acquisition has embraced heavy linen, the colour of double cream, from the market in Isle-sur-la-Sorgue (one can never have enough tablecloths); kaftans from Morocco; beadwork by Masai women: the colours were irresistible; and a Zulu ceremonial head-dress that looks marvellous in the hall. The six chinoiserie chairs from the Compton Turrets sale are enchanting, even though two are broken. But does one really have more than four to supper in the kitchen?

Of course Cornelia doesn't need a blackamoor candelabra, but he was seductively lurking in an antique shop she passed in Cornwall. And heavens, they had some pretty plates. Cornelia doesn't believe in matching china; her table is a chipped *mélange* of armorial, Provençal and Italian pottery. Little bits of *famille rose*, filled with fresh figs, dot surfaces not already covered with treen, lapis lazuli eggs and ornamental birdcages. It's so practical having lots of pictures as it saves on wallpaper. Anyone unwise enough to open a cupboard will be deluged with old *Country Life*s and *Tatler*s. 'But darling, I never know when I might need to look something up.' Sitting is hazardous because of the Steiff teddies. 'You surely can't begrudge Growler a chair.' Cornelia's husband has long since retreated to his library and the whisky decanter. He wistfully thinks 'Cornelia's Cornucopia' would be a perfect name for a junk shop.

The Pub Bore

VINCE IS FURIOUS, which is quite mild for him. Round about the time of Gordon Brown's budgets he is positively apoplectic. Don't get him going on stealth taxes, or the money being thrown at the NHS just so that his Auntie Winnie could lie on a trolley in a filthy corridor. 'She was there 16 hours, without so much as a bedpan.' Vince is a stickler for lurid detail. Unwary patrons of the Fur and Feathers have been caught with Aunt Winnie's NHS Drama Episode 2: The State of the Toilets. It is not an appetising prelude to a cheese and pickle sandwich and a quiet pint.

The problem is that Vince's sacrosanct spot at the bar, by the Old Muckspreader real ale, is bang in the middle, so he's unavoidable. Couples chatting quietly while mine host fetches a stiff whisky and a glass of white wine are suddenly interrupted by Vince saying, 'I think you've got that wrong.' They should not take this personally. Everybody's views are wrong compared with Vince's. Particularly on illegal immigrants, benefit fraud and street crime. His Uncle Fred (husband of the unfortunate Aunt Winnie) was mugged by a youth in trainers wearing a hoodie. 'They do that so they can't be caught on the CCTV cameras – hoodies should be made illegal.' Vince is definitely not for faint-hearted liberals, nor anyone with a refined sense of humour. After the fourth pint, and having expended deranged loathing on all politicians except George Bush ('He's got the right idea – nuke the bastards'), Vince may tell a joke. This is a serpentine process, encouraged by the pub's remnants who are in their cups, and culminating in Vince saying, 'Let's see, now what is the punchline?' to collective groaning. It's more appreciation than he gets at home where the wife can't bear him shouting at Tony Blair on the telly.

Vince is definitely not for faint-hearted liberals

*Lavender and Rosemary are amongst serried ranks of literary fans
with Iris Murdoch haircuts*

The Literary Festival Devotees

LAVENDER AND ROSEMARY have been to them all: Hay-on-Wye, Bath, Cheltenham, and they eagerly await the delights of Folkestone. The spartan premises of drill halls across the land are as nirvana when enhanced by the presence of Antony Beevor or Sebastian Faulks. Lavender and Rosemary thrill to Beevor's glossy bossiness; they faint over Faulks. Max Hastings's approach to modern history is a thrilling call to arms.

Each morning at their b & b, over muesli and the *Guardian G2* section, Lavender and Rosemary plan their day, stabbing at the festival programme with a pencil. They will have to be very early for Alexander McCall Smith: serried ranks of fans with Iris Murdoch haircuts will be queuing to worship at his shrine. Lavender and Rosemary dote on *The No.1 Ladies' Detective Agency* and are saving up for a trip to Botswana. Lavender has put on her best top. In bilious yellow, it has unfortunate overtones of tie-dye, and her bosom is somewhat flapping in the wind. Both she and Rosemary favour the three-quarter-length baggy trouser, but neither exfoliation nor St Tropez fake tan has graced their blue-white legs. The callused toe is a symbol of intellectual rigour. Pedicures do not correspond with a fervour for the Orange Prize for fiction; Rosemary's most extravagant concession to fashion is some African trading beads, frequently augmented by spectacles on strings adorned with feathers and seed pods. Finally, at the top of the queue for the divine McCall Smith, they will fish battered copies of *In the Company of Cheerful Ladies* out of fringed hessian bags and say, 'Do you mind awfully signing my paperback?'

*Eliza is convinced that none of the amusing people
will find her amusing*

The Shy Woman

EMBARRASSMENT HAS CAUSED Eliza to tie her body into a figure of eight. She really wanted to come to the Coningsbys' party, they always have such amusing people – isn't that Julian Fellowes by the armoire? – but now she is actually here she would rather be anywhere else. Convinced that none of the amusing people will find her in the least amusing, Eliza attempts to melt into a dim corner of the room, hoovers up a bowl of peanuts and drinks her champagne rather too quickly. That she is dressed in orchid-bright exotica belies the melting stance; Eliza aspires to glamour despite her demeanour conspiring against her. Yet men feel sorry for her, and bring more champagne. Chippy Bunce says to Adrian Cordite that it's jolly refreshing to see a woman who doesn't have her tits slapped out like turbots on Harrods' fish counter. 'Good sort, old Eliza, she was at school with my sister Anthea. Eliza listens to me banging on about stockbroking, which is more than any of these supermodel types around here do.'

Little does Chippy know that underneath Eliza's benign ropes of pearls beats a heart bursting with fury that no one ever asks her about her job at a theatrical agency. That she has a really interesting time babysitting nascent Colin Firths. Meanwhile, she is listening to Adrian droning on about *The Producers*. 'Absolutely marvellous,' he's saying, his Adam's apple bobbing up and down excitedly. And Eliza is thinking that *The Producers* is absolutely the sort of theatre for people who don't go to the theatre. She's now rather tipsy, which makes her seem sweet and insecure. Anthea Bunce goes past and hisses at her brother, 'Remember what Mummy said: being shy is only a way of drawing attention to yourself.'

The Prep School Head

MR DAWSON IS a hero to the mothers. None will forget the First Term, when he provided vast gin and tonics, plus boxes of Kleenex, as they left their Harrys, Archies and Olivers at St Horrid's. 'Cheer up, Lady Lucinda, we're not Hogwart's but neither are we Dotheboys Hall. Archie will only be beaten twice daily with barbed wire. Hah-hah! Just my little joke, Mrs Sherrin. Another Kleenex? I feel sure that Ollie is going to be a huge asset to us and I think that he and Pipsqueak Minor were at Wetherby together, were they not?' His Labradors are a great comfort to the homesick. It takes the first match to shake the parents down. The children are easy. Mr Dawson, who pretends he's not known as 'Duffer', takes football himself, still in his old Eton socks. The boys are a bit in awe because Duffer has climbed K2 (the mothers raised all his sponsorship for charity), is running the London marathon and taking Form 2B white-water rafting in Colorado. Duffer, while observing the tiresome new Health & Safety regs, is damned if they're going to interfere with geography field trips in Wales or Outward Bound epics.

He has an enthusiasm matched only by that of his Labradors, and a disciplinary code based on the three Rs, hard work and proper values. Duffer Dawson is in favour of team sports; Mary 'Muffy' Dawson is in favour of proper food. She's joined at the hip with Jamie Oliver in subverting school dinners with vegetables and fruit. Duffy and Muffy are running a tight ship at St Horrid's with firm tolerance, albeit that Mr Dawson's life is measured out in orange segments at half-time. On their holidays they explore Italian churches, staying in modest *pensiones*. Lady Lucinda tells all her friends with hopeful children that there's no one like Dawson for instilling old-fashioned decency and manners into their little brutes.

Duffer Dawson is in favour of the three Rs,
hard work and team sports

Millicent is a fervent believer that golf, like measles,
should be caught young

The Lady Golfer

FOR SOME, GIDEON is their bible but Millicent Trubshawe's source
of spiritual sustenance is the Royal and Ancient rulebook. Golf
has been her religion ever since she caddied for her father during
bracing Scottish holidays. As the wind whistled off the heather, there
was nothing sunnier than the chip-shot holed. Millicent is a fervent
believer that golf, like measles, should be caught young. Now if she's
not playing golf, she's thinking about it. Or watching it, having
obtained Sky Sports for pigging out on the tournaments. The
children are all grown up, Peter is perfectly happy pottering in the
garden, so she plays three times a week and has a handicap of 19,
which Daddy would consider respectable without being showy.

Her generous interest in the younger members, even caddying for
them in tournaments and dispensing bananas to keep up their energy
levels, does not extend to scantily clad female golf enthusiasts
sunbathing on the fairway in the hope that Hugh Grant might
be playing a round. Whoever would have thought there would be
hussies at Swindale? Nor is she entirely convinced by the new
banker-lawyer lady members wearing Chanel jackets and talking
a little too loudly about their interlocking grip at the summer
barbecue. Millicent's daughter gave her a Fendi beige leather golf
bag for Christmas, but the nearest she ever intends to get to fashion's
cutting edge is her electric golf trolley. The battery is the weight of
an elephant, and when it breaks down on the course it can't be
moved. Others of its ilk stand deserted, making it look as if Swindale
has been invaded by stalled Daleks, proof that technology is horribly
suspect. It has reunited Millicent with Nigel the caddy – now they're
working on her strategy for the winter sun tournament in Egypt.
The most intriguing thing she's ever heard about the Valley of the
Kings is that it has a golf course.

The Long Lunchers

CLEMENT AND DULCIE meet once a week at Royce's, out of which they can roll home to a splendid evening of novels, *Coronation Street*, and no necessity for nourishment other than a stiff whisky. Royce's suits them perfectly – starched napkins that crack like whips, proper English food and very few young people. Clement and Dulcie do not wish to sit next to some girl the width of a breadstick, drinking mineral water. It would quite take the edge off the excellent claret Clement has ordered. Dulcie always has a glass of champagne to dispel the rigours of writing book reviews since 6am; and should they have the oak-smoked salmon to start with there's a very good case for a couple of glasses of Pouilly-Fumé.

Clement is normally a roast of the day man, but autumn brings the gamy allure of grouse and partridge, so fortifying after a morning spent pounding out his wine column on an ancient Smith-Corona. The P key is missing, which makes the Pomerols very tough on his middle finger. Neither Clement nor Dulcie has anything to do with computers, mobile telephones or Government guidelines on alcohol units. When Dulcie was taken out to lunch by some rascally publisher, and he ordered half a bottle of burgundy, she said kindly that it was marvellous for her but what was he having? Clement has never heard of cholesterol, and would like buttery mash, extra bread sauce and creamed spinach with his grouse, please. As well as the Brussels sprouts and the straw potatoes. Nothing wrong with a good feed; it'll be a near-run thing between the bread-and-butter pudding and the Welsh rarebit. Clement is inordinately fond of savouries. Preferably followed by a cigar and a glass of port. They both find that coffee interferes with sleeping in the afternoons.

*Neither Clement nor Dulcie has any time
for Government guidelines on alcohol units*

Pamela can tie a bowline knot in three seconds

The Sailing Wife

PAMELA IS THE first lady commodore of the Blimpton-on-Sea Yacht Club. Her bracing attitude, salty as a sea breeze, has resulted in Jane Churchill curtains for the Club Room and a new pontoon for the Wavemaker 30 boats. Pamela has been a terrific proselytiser for the Wavemakers. Other clubs have their Redwings or their Mermaids, thus she was determined that Blimpton should also have a one-design class. There were mutterings in the woodwork of the old membership about plastic boats, and Pamela's mild-mannered husband, Ronald, really preferred sailing in his old wooden Dragon, but all have had to admit that the Wavemakers have been a success. The class got several mentions in the sports pages during Cowes Week; swathed in Henri Lloyd oilskins, Pamela helmed her boat to win, and achieved the nirvana of having tea on the Royal Yacht Squadron lawn. Her smile was so radiant it seemed as if her teeth had been whitened to match her pearls. Now she is running the annual GUSTO course – Grown Up Sailing Training. Potential sailing wives, with voluminous bottoms and new Docksiders, are intimidated from the outset by being addressed as Down-From-Fulham Girls – 'Don't make the mistake of thinking when I shout "Leo" it means DiCaprio' – and Pamela's ability to tie a bowline knot in three seconds.

Meanwhile Pamela's daughter, Linnet, is teaching the DFF children in their Optimists, little boats-in-the-bath called *Lollipop* and *Snoopy*. Ronald is faintly bemused that he has spawned this legion of women. Just when he thought they might have a gentle cruise in balmy Mediterranean waters, Pamela is organising the Blimpton-on-Sea rally off the west coast of Scotland. Naturally Ronald is frightfully proud of the old girl's organisational skills, but he sometimes wonders if she's going to turn into a navy-blue battleship.

The Road Rager

ALBERT'S NEAREST AND dearest would not recognise the florid pustule of aggression now threatening Mr Stoat, a timid parish councillor. At home Albert is a model paterfamilias, patting small grandchildren on downy heads, and treating the wife to a slap-up do at the Badger and Mole on her birthday. It is only when he gets behind a wheel that he becomes a teeth-grinding, wheel-gripping, engine-revving, horn-tooting paroxysm of fury. Every other benighted soul on the road is a fool and a charlatan. 'Did you see that? Did you *see* that?' is his mantra to himself as a white-van man shoots the lights, or a blonde in a 4x4 turns left when she's indicated right. Double-parked school-run mothers are a particular heart-attack zone.

Mr Stoat's crime is to have hesitated at the intersection, uncertain in which part of Daisy Lane lies the barn conversion he has to check for plastic windows. Albert roared up the lane on a mission for his plumbing business, and 'nearly bloody rammed you in the bum, you git'. This is not the terminology of parish council meetings; Mr Stoat has locked his car door with a shaking hand. Since a file on his passenger seat marked 'Mr Les Stoat, Parish Councillor' has betrayed his calling to the life-threatening force outside, he is now enduring a fusillade on being an interfering little twerp what makes life impossible for those in the building trade to make an honest living. Spittle is hitting the windscreen. 'It's people like you, dithering little tinpot Hitlers, who cause accidents.' Only the queue building up behind the ill-matched combatants frustrates Albert's incipient tirade against the entire Government and its nannying regulations. Telling Mr Stoat he's a right little plonker, and kicking his tyre, Albert returns to his Ford Warrior. He enjoyed that.

Albert is a teeth-grinding paroxysm of fury

*Romilly's closeness reminds Pinker of a course he did
at Sandhurst on interrogating the enemy*

The Space Invader

ROMILLY HAS DRIVEN Pinker Ackroyd to the wall. As she moves ever closer, all he can see is a set of teeth with hot champagne breath and the remains of a cocktail sausage in a left molar. It isn't a mouth, it's a food trap. As it opens and shuts, Pinker fixates on the blackish half moon where Romilly's crown meets the gummy bit. They have done the party waltz, her moving inexorably forward, Pinker stepping back until the room ran out, and now he's tonsil-deep in enforced intimacy. 'So, Pinker, how *are* you?' Romilly is saying, and the ghastly thing is that she actually wants to know. Pinker is reminded of a course on interrogating the enemy that he did at Sandhurst. His eyes dart desperately from side to side, like a small, dull antelope cornered by a lioness in the Masai Mara.

Romilly is now asking about his children: 'Can it really be Marcus I hear on the World Service, reporting from Eritrea? I can remember when he won the egg and spoon race at Thomas's.' Romilly's power of recall is unnatural. She is now interrogating Pinker about his knee operation. 'You always go to King Edward VII, don't you? I came to visit you when you had your prostate done, and you were frightfully cross because your sister Cicely had sent you orange dahlias.' This is eerie. Pinker feels as if Romilly is invading his soul, let alone knowing an excessive amount about his body. She is now asking what he has been to see lately at the National Theatre – 'Wasn't *The History Boys* marvellous?' – and how compelling he must be finding the theatre of war – 'Or is it attrition?' – in Iraq. Pinker is panic-stricken as Romilly's crystalline blue contact lenses bore into him. Suddenly, she is gone, saying, 'Pinker, so lovely to see you, but we didn't really talk.'

'Nothing must go on before the lights; this is a man's job'

The Christmas Tree Decorators

IT IS A scene of savage recrimination and regret. 'Who put the bloody lights away last year?' is bellowed through the house as Julian struggles with the traditional Gordian knot of Christmas festivity. 'Who was the blithering idiot? I've told you all year after year to put the fairy lights back in the boxes correctly.' Xanthe is livid. Of all the things guaranteed to engender post-Christmas gloom syndrome, it would be sticking myriad little bulbs into those cardboard slots like serrated teeth. 'Anyway, they never fit. Why don't *you* do it, Mr Fusspot? If you were any more controlling you'd invade Poland.' Julian takes the moral high ground about having to return to work 'to pay for this nightmare of extravagance. The least you and the children could do is put the decorations away properly.'

All teenagers have disappeared with the get-a-life-Dad eye-roll, and plugged themselves into their iPods. The tree is listing to port, which necessitates pit-propping with logs; Xanthe is in heavy-duty Marigolds because she's allergic to pine needles; and the dog makes his disapproval of the seasonal ill-will entirely clear. The stepladder, essential to Operation Christmas Fairy, has to be retrieved from the garage in pouring rain. A charming attempt by Molly, aged eight, to attach gingerbread men to the lower branches is repulsed by Julian shouting, 'Nothing, but nothing must go on before the lights. This is a man's job, we have to have winding not plonking.' An extension lead is required, and adaptor plugs for countless sets of twinkling cheer. The set that pulses to Christmas carols does a tinny 'Silent Night' and dies. Julian spends all evening with hands thrust in the tree to find the aberrant bulb that's got loose.

The Mail-Order Addict

NATALIE DIDN'T REALLY mean to buy the black rubber gloves studded with faux jewels and trimmed with feather boa – so practical for the Christmas melée of washing up – but they were irresistible. Only £6.99 in the Gift-U-Like catalogue and surely a witty alternative to the scented candle as a present for Ruby? The bunny slippers meant for Aunt Bunny from Presents 'R' Us have been appropriated by the dog, so she'll have to have the mink hot-water bottle cover with a satin bow. Even Natalie cannot imagine why she ordered cashmere lavender-scented angels hand-made in pink and lilac, but they'll be marvellous for the vicar's wife. Having wrapped them in Midnight Owls in a Snowy Landscape paper from Animal Magic, it would be advisable not to confuse the package with the Kama Sutra pop-up book, £9.99 from Original Ideas, intended for cousin Sid. Nor should the Pope Soap-on-a-Rope, 'guaranteed to wash away your sins', be given to Phyllis, who's converted to Catholicism.

Of course Natalie means to throw all the catalogues away, but she can't resist a peek. It's mesmeric. What about the chocolate Labrador filled with solid chocolate bones 'made from the prized cocoa beans of Java', despite not having a Labrador? Or the ironing-board cover with a full-length picture of Jordan, whose bikini vanishes when hot? That should get Harry to do the ironing. Harry says that if Natalie orders one more electric pepper mill which he has to collect from the bloody sorting office – requiring ID befitting a terrorist suspect – he's off. And that was before the Ear-Vac. Natalie fell victim to this nifty suction solution to ear wax – despite not having any – on its buy-one-get-one-free allure. She's never been able to send anything back in 28 days if not absolutely delighted.

*Natalie means to throw all the catalogues away,
but can't resist a peek*

'It'll be such fun to see how everyone looks now we're all a hundred'

The School Reunion

HENRIETTA DIDN'T REALLY want to go to Founder's Day. Then Sukie rang her up and said, 'Come on Henry, it's St Mary's centenary and it'll be such fun to see how everyone looks now we're all a hundred. Must go and get my Botox topped up. Byeee!' It is a long time since anyone called Henrietta Henry, and she'd felt a pang of nostalgia for the panelled refectory and the walled garden where she'd read *Lady Chatterley's Lover*. Now she's being interrogated by a woman wearing Country Casuals. 'Henry? Remember me? Inky. Inky Stiffkey, although now I'm Ramsbottom.' Henrietta is not convinced this is an improvement. 'Well, Henry, you're so thin, you haven't been ill have you? It's our age, of course. Things Happen. But I hear you are a great success – now what is it you do exactly?' Inky's note of interrogative disbelief makes Henry feel exactly as if she was back in Mother Violet's study, being berated about her geog homework.

There's Weed, severe in a hairband, and now a High Court judge; there's Moth, just the same, bless her, a little grey around the edges, but radiating the sunny good sense that made her head girl. 'I'm still teaching, despite all this ridiculous PC stuff. Most of the time you want to wallop the little beasts and nowadays we're not allowed to tell parents their darlings are dimwits – educational guidelines. Look, there's Blossom, she's now our leading expert in genetic research.' And what about Tonks, who always had one sock down and ran in the corridors? She's a gynaecologist. As Mother Bell gets up to speak – 'Silence everyone, this is Ding-Dong here' – Henrietta looks around the tweeded bosoms, the miasma of blue mascara, the blondes with divorces but a mission in charity work, and sees women of achievement. She's glad she came.

As a pedestrian, she despises all cars

The Pedestrian

IVY HAS THE divine right of way. As a pedestrian, she despises all cars, stepping out with the blind faith of self-righteousness. Drivers, brakes screaming at the zebra crossing, loathe her with a fury especially reserved for the ambulatory and innocent who are impeding their progress to terribly important lunches. It is Ivy's hand, held out with a morally superior 'Stop!' gesture, that makes blondes in Chelsea tractors bite the steering wheel. Who is this eco-geeko getting between them and their highlights at Neville? Ivy is, naturally, on her way to an energy awareness group. A mature student, she is doing a Masters degree in conservation. Endless seminars about making the world a better place in which to live haven't resulted in anything practical, like helping old ladies across the road. Ivy's pedestrian ethics consist of self-preservation with a sneer. She looks right, left and right again, but having her nose in the air means that small children frequently get trodden on, and sticks kicked from the tremulous hands of blind men.

Only the bicyclists, sneaking up silently around the corner of a clear road, constitute a threat to her equilibrium. Left flailing in the gutter, Ivy shouts, 'Bloody bicyclists!' and the bicyclist ripostes, 'Bloody pedestrians!' so that honour is satisfied between two of the smuggest users of the Queen's highway. 'I always walk,' is what Ivy says when she arrives, beetroot in the face, at parties, and people kindly enquire if she's quite well. 'If people walked more we wouldn't have an obesity problem,' she adds, helping herself liberally to canapés. She's so oxygenated that the white wine whizzes to her head and Teddy Flitbat has to drive her home. On the way, a woman steps out into the road, the brakes squeal and Ivy, secure in the leather embrace of the Toyota Amazon, hiccups, 'Bloody pedestrians.'

The Magazine Obsessives

CECI AND MIKE are suicidal. To cheer themselves up in the dank, drippy hellhole that is February they've bought all the magazines in what was supposed to be an orgy of indulgence equivalent to a box of chocolates. Instead, they are poignantly reminded of all their inadequacies. There's no miraculous detox cure which includes beer; to lose 10lb in 10 days involves disgusting horrors like green tea, which Mike tried last year. It tasted like urine then, and he has no confidence that anything has changed now. Ceci has again discovered that she wasn't invited to any of the best parties and that 'everyone wearing Juicy Couture' does not include her. (Also that green, in which she's invested heavily, is so last year.)

She and Mike live in Putney, an aberration among the *Design for Living* statistics that 'everyone' is living alone, nor does Putney figure as a fashionable neighbourhood in which 'everyone' is living; it is depressingly tainted by its proximity to Wandsworth, referred to as Nappy Valley, which serves to remind Ceci and Mike that they have no designer baby. Mike, who has just transformed their bedroom into the cream dream, courtesy of Dulux, is devastated by the news that wallpaper is back. Ceci's New Year's resolution was to rustle up divine dinner parties, but friends, Alan the accountant and Edith the estate agent, hardly equate with Hugh and Jemima in terms of *Tattle*'s most-wanted guests. One small ray of sunshine is Brad and Jen's split (six pages in *OK!* magazine), so even into the life of the blessed some rain does fall. Ceci is going to put on the free face pack provided with *Glamour*, and go to bed with *Vogue*. Mike wonders if he could get an Eames chair on eBay and whether it would change his life. The dog doesn't understand why they do it to themselves.

Magazines poignantly remind them of all their inadequacies

Antonia is phoning for 'a catch-up' about innovative concepts at the Sloth Hotel

The PR Blonde

ANTONIA IS DEAD perky. This morning she is following up the e-mail that she followed up with a letter about an innovative concept at the Sloth Hotel. 'Hello? Is that *Gloss* magazine? This is Antonia from Dimwit PR. Could I speak to your restaurant critic please?' Journalists hide under their desks, mouthing desperately that they are out. None has yet recovered from Antonia's press release describing 'why it is so exciting that the Sloth has 700 vintage wines and its own somalia'. Even by Antonia's standards of 'unique opportunities', a viticultural war zone is unusual. The spelling bee and the correct use of the apostrophe have merrily passed Antonia by on the other side; her synthetic enthusiasm is suited to the laptop presentation, with which she can bring a pleasant drinks party to a shuddering halt. As she claps her hands and tosses her hair, there's a pitiful shuffling towards the exit, but Nicola, Dimwit's door blonde, has cut off the retreat from flashing Apple Mac images of Swankarama's new development in the Cayman Islands, with its 18-hole golf course designed by Norman Pringle.

The imprisoned throng are bombarded with information about the spa's square footage 'incorporating the philosophy of feng shui', and Antonia is particularly perky (flick-flick of the highlights) about the Swankarama's romantic bath menu: 'The bath is surrounded by ylang-ylang candles and filled with rose petals – it's pink and bubbly, and that's just the champagne!' Her style is to speak in exclamation marks, madly irritating to the freelance writers she inevitably telephones at home for 'a catch-up' when they've got a plumbing crisis, or are trying to de-nit their children. 'I just want to tell you about Juicy's new lipgloss in the flavour of Sarah Jessica Parker's favourite cocktail at the Pizazz Bar. It's called Suck Off!' How too, too blonde.

The Divorced Couple

IT IS THE Saturday handover. Giles and Camilla hover on the doorstep, smiling thinly. He does not come into the house they once shared, but over Camilla's rigid shoulders he can see all that is familiar and in the past – also that she has replaced the portrait of his grandfather with an alarmingly modern picture. On the principle that less is more (and when did the Camilla he knew become a one-green-apple-on-a-white-canvas sort of person?), it looks expensive. That settlement was ruinous; and now he clocks the Hermès bag on the hall table. Bloody hell. Camilla, who's put the bag there deliberately, is giving clipped instructions about E-numbers. 'Here at home,' heavy emphasis on home, 'Rollo has no Coca-Cola, or chocolate, Giles. The Es make him hyper. At *home* he has organic food.' Camilla bitterly suspects that Samantha, who was her best friend until she ran off with Giles, thinks organic is a permutation of orgasm.

Nor is she best pleased that Giles has given Rollo a GameBoy. 'You can't buy his love, you know,' she hisses. Little annoys her more than the child bouncing on the sofa on Saturday mornings chanting, 'Daddy's coming! Daddy's coming!' Then the emptiness in the house when the hyper-whirlwind has gone to the happy land of pizza and DVDs, where his Egypt project will be left festering in his suitcase despite Camilla's veiled exhortations to his father: 'Daddy will help you with your project, darling. You will, won't you, Giles? It has to be in on Monday. Hugo Pswot's father actually took him to the pyramids; some daddies are so dedicated.' Giles accelerates away before the mummies in the British Museum are tendered. A bug-eyed Rollo is returned to the doorstep buffer zone on Sunday evening. Camilla stays up until 2am making a pyramid out of an organic muesli packet.

*Over Camilla's rigid shoulders Giles sees all that's familiar
and past in the house they once shared*

Gerrie has thrived on the manifestation of human degeneration that is reality TV

The Television Intellectual

EVER SINCE GERALDINE sprang from Liverpool in the 1960s, she has been a totem of populist culture. The Beatles, Cilla, Roger McGough – Gerrie Stilgoe was at the eye of the revolutionary storm in her leather mini-skirt and false eyelashes. Or so she liked everyone to think. That she was actually brought up in the shamingly middle-class environs of Altrincham and went to the local grammar has mercifully been lost in time. Her era at Oxford was as a Zuleika with a John Lennon accent; she interviewed the lost Beatle, Stuart Whatshisname, in Hamburg for *Isis*. She said Kafka was crap and *Coronation Street* was where it was at. Her paper, 'The Soap Stigma', was subsequently taught at Warwick University. During *Dallas* she outed academics who'd abandoned Suetonius for Sue Ellen. *Friends* and *Frasier* inspired a new career surge; her book *Stiletto Empowerment* deconstructed *Sex and the City*.

And then the gift of reality television. Gerrie has thrived on the manifestation of human degeneration that the *Big Brother* house implies. The 21st century, she's declared gleefully, is going to be 100 years of the moron. Her television show *Uterus: The Womb with a View* has gorged on *I'm a Celebrity*. Gerrie declares herself a devotee of Tanya in *Footballers' Wives* 'and all those glossy bints who've got more balls than footballers have ever kicked'. The Stilgoe rant is beloved of television producers; she can be relied upon to lambast Cherie's absurd attempts at style, while being revisionist on Emma Thompson's hair extensions. The fact that the actress went braless at the age of 44 (and was criticised for it by Amanda Platell) is enough to elevate her as a feminist icon, 'even if the awards ceremonies she attends are meaningless crap'. Not that Gerrie is one to turn down presenting any of them.

The Over-Attentive
Shop Assistant

SHEREEN IS TERRIFYING Valerie Pargeter, who does not want to be told that she'd look marvellous in taupe. Besides, the object Shereen is holding in her talons looks alarmingly like chainmail. Shereen – fixed smile, gummy teeth – glitters with misinformation. 'Chainmail, Madam? I think we can hardly call Pierre Sauvage's design anything so retro. Here we have cutting edge.' As Shereen rattles the tectonic plates of this repulsive garment, Valerie is uncertain whether she's supposed to be reassured, but suspects she is being patronised. Shereen has not intimidated the unconfident in Fayre Lady without results. Many times have Boden-clad mothers nipped in after the school run 'just to have a look'. But Shereen doesn't do 'just looking', and they've slunk out with carrier bags of Sauvage nightmare, driven to their credit cards by her trilling through the changing room, 'Shall I bring you a size 16?' Even as brittle, thin women browse through the MaxMara trouser suits, Shereen – batting eyelashes like individually applied spider's legs – stalks them along the rails, purring that camel is a marvellous colour for autumn.

Those caught in Shereen's unblinking gaze are eerily reminded of Carole Caplin. Only a rub-down with crystals in the Downing Street shower could equal the embarrassment of Shereen bursting upon the undressed in their greying underwear. Running scream-ing from Fayre Lady naked is a possible alternative, but instead the cowed find themselves standing meekly before Shereen as she cocoons a too-small, too-revealing magenta shift dress in tissue. 'Madam will look just like Jackie Kennedy at the Christmas party this year.'

'Shall I bring you a size 16?'

The Brat

MATILDA IS ALWAYS allowed to answer the telephone. Isn't she clever? ''ello, dis ees Tilda, woo are woo?' People are desperately confused as to whether they've rung the loony bin or got Jake and Sophia's Filipina maid. It is only when Matilda says, 'I was 'ick in Dada's Pawsha 'en I 'ent to Mimi's party dwessed as a faiwy' that the plumber realises he's talking to the little beast who hid his wrench in her toy box. 'Can I speak to Daddy, please, dearie?' he says, thinking that it's weird how the posh people let their kids run riot, and he'd never let his Tracey be an answering service. Deadly silence, followed by a dial tone, indicate that Matilda has got bored and waddled off to torture her puppy.

If anyone had told Jake and Sophia that they would be the sort of parents who let their child redecorate restaurants with ketchup, they'd have died. They are *Independent*-reading architects who looked askance when their friends' children dropped jam on the stainless-steel Bulthaup. Now they talk of little else but laissez-faire parenting. Dinner parties were entertained by Matilda's first word: 'No-boo'. Tinkly laugh from Sophia. 'Tilda's first solid food was the black cod with miso, you know.' Then there was the sequel of the joined-up sentence ('I's 'ad a poo') and the importance of familial bonding. This means they all sleep in the same bed in acute discomfort, if, that is, Matilda ever goes to bed. Jake and Sophia feel she must make her own choices, so she's still running around, screaming with exhaustion, at 10 o'clock. When her parents took her to the opening of the new Saatchi exhibition, many thought Matilda should be pickled in formaldehyde. She kicked Sophia on the shins and Sophia said, 'I can tell you're angry. Why are you angry with Mummy?' The other guests thought it was nothing a good sharp slap wouldn't sort out.